MIRACLES IN THE MEADOW

BUTTERFLY FIELD FARM ANIMAL SANCTUARY

21 INSPIRATIONAL STORIES OF RESCUED AND REDEEMED ANIMALS

LARRY RANDOLPH

MIRACLES IN THE MEADOW

Larry Randolph
Miracles in the Meadow

All rights reserved
Copyright © 2025 by Larry Randolph

No part of this publication may be reproduced, distributed, or transmitted
in any form or by any means, including photocopying, recording, or other
electronic or mechanical methods, without the prior written permission of
the publisher, except in the case of brief quotations embodied in critical
reviews and certain other noncommercial uses permitted by copyright law.

Published by Spines

ISBN: 979-8-89691-475-4

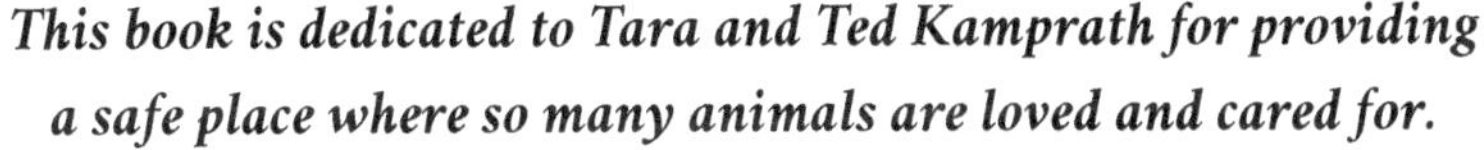

This book is dedicated to Tara and Ted Kamprath for providing a safe place where so many animals are loved and cared for.

Thank you for your gentle hearts and unwavering love as you so diligently care for each soul.

You have embraced each one with open arms, providing them with a forever home of peace and tranquility.

God smiles down on you as you care for His beloved.

INTRODUCTION
THE BACKSTORY - A HAVEN OF HOPE AND GRACE IN THE FIELDS

"I look up to the mountains. Does my help come from there? My help comes from the Lord, who made heaven and earth." Psalm 121:1-2

In the autumn of 2016, Tara and Ted Kamprath, accompanied by their two young daughters, Jessie and Sophie and a loyal canine companion, Bella, exchanged their busy lives in Tampa, Florida, for the serene embrace of Bedford, Virginia. Drawn to the allure of the Blue Ridge Mountains and the tranquil rhythm of rural life, they established their home on a picturesque five-acre parcel, where rolling hills are rich and lush and breathtaking vistas unfolded before them. They had found refuge in the beauty of God's creation. In this little piece of heaven, they felt a deep connection with their Creator. Each day was filled with gratitude for the beauty around them and the peace that only God can provide. For several years, their existence was marked by stability of fulfilling careers, the joy of raising spirited twin girls, and a profound appreciation for their picturesque sanctuary.

Yet, an unseen hand was at work, quietly reshaping their hearts and minds. As if guided by divine providence, a pivotal moment arrived during a vegetarian festival in Richmond, Virginia, in the fall of 2019. Amidst the vibrant displays, their attention was captured by the plight of rescued farm animals—pot-bellied pigs, goats, donkeys, huge cows, mini horses and many other blind and disabled animals whose gentle eyes seemed to mirror their own yearning for compassion. A profound shift occurred within them; a seed of empathy was sown, taking root in the fertile soil of their spirits.

Inspired by a growing awareness of the suffering endured by countless animals destined for slaughter, Tara and Ted embarked on a journey of discovery. They delved into a world previously unknown to them, a realm where vulnerability and resilience coexisted. Their hearts, overflowing with love and compassion, were stirred to action. Through prayer and introspection, they discerned a divine calling to establish a sanctuary, a haven where these gentle beings could find refuge, healing and redemption.

Thus, in December 2019, Butterfly Field Farm Animal Sanctuary was born. Acres of land were transformed into a haven, where fences and barns emerged as symbols of hope and protection. The sanctuary's establishment coincided with the acquisition of 501(c)(3) nonprofit status, a formal commitment to their mission. Word of their sanctuary spread rapidly, and soon, an influx of desperate pleas arrived, each a poignant testament to the urgent need for sanctuary. In a matter of months, the farm became home to nearly thirty animals, a diverse family united by shared experiences of adversity.

As the sanctuary flourished, Ted felt a compelling urge to devote himself entirely to his newfound calling. Resigning from his previous occupation, he embraced the role of full-time farmer and caregiver, tending to the growing community of over a hundred animals who now thrived under his watchful eye.

Reflecting on their extraordinary journey, Tara and Ted find profound resonance in the words of Proverbs 3:5-6,

"Trust in the Lord with all your heart and do not depend on your own understanding. Seek his will in all you do, and he will show you which path to take."

Their unwavering faith and trust in the Lord have been their steadfast companion, guiding them through challenges and illuminating their path. Butterfly Field Farm Animal Sanctuary stands as a living testament of redemption, a place where the wounds of the past are gently tended and where a new chapter of love and freedom unfolds and a new beginning has been given. Each time we choose to act with kindness to God's animals, we reflect God's word in Proverbs 12:10,

"The godly care for their animals, but the wicked are always cruel."

The sanctuary of Butterfly Field Farm is a beautiful example of compassion, grace and hope and serves as an inspiration to all those who encounter it.

Sophie, Ted, Tara, Jessie

A DIVINE RESCUE:
HOPE FOR THE HOPELESS/FREDERICK AND RICHARD

"I tell you the truth, when you did it to one of the least of these, my brothers and sisters, you were doing it to me."

— MATTHEW 25:40

IN THE HEART of Butterfly Field Farm Animal Sanctuary, a tale of compassion unfolds a testament to the boundless love of God. Frederick and Richard, also lovingly known as the "Blind Boys," are two magnificent creatures who found their sanctuary amidst life's challenges. Frederick, a 600 lb. Barringer steer, was born into darkness, his world shrouded in perpetual night. His physical form bore the marks of a life touched by disabilities, yet his spirit was a beacon of gentleness. As the scriptures proclaim, "The Lord is good to everyone; he has compassion on all his creation" Psalm 145:9. Frederick, though challenged, embodied this divine compassion, radiating love and acceptance.

At 900 lb. Richard also is a Barringer steer, and he too,

faced his own trials. Once blessed with sight, Pink Eye robbed him of his precious vision. If only his previous owner had medicated Richard's Pink Eye, he would not have lost his ability to see. It is a lesson that when you are the guardian of an animal, one needs to take responsibility to give that animal the very best care. Yet, even in the dimness, his soul remains bright. As the Bible reminds us:

"The Lord is close to the brokenhearted and rescues those whose spirits are crushed."

— PSALM 34:18

Richard's journey mirrored this verse, showcasing resilience and an unbroken spirit.

In God's perfect plan, Sarah, a compassionate soul, became their guardian angel. She lived close to the farm where Frederick and Richard lived, and after witnessing their disabilities and struggles, she felt a divine calling to rescue them. For you see, she watched every day as the large herd of beef cows pushed Frederick and Richard away from the hay and did not allow them to eat. They were losing weight and becoming extremely thin. She had to do something as her heart ached for these two beautiful boys. Her actions echoed the words of Proverbs 31:8,

"You have not handed me over to my enemies but have set me in a safe place."

Sarah's determination led them to Butterfly Field Farm, a haven of love and care. Praise God for Sarah. Shouldn't we all strive to be like her?

Their arrival was marked by fear and uncertainty. Yet, with unwavering faith, the sanctuary team navigated the challenges.

"Trust in the Lord with all your heart and do not depend on your own understanding. Seek his will in all you do, and he will show you which path to take."

— PROVERBS 3:5-6

At first, Frederick and Richard were terrified of their new surroundings and only walked in a very tight circle in the pasture. Little by little, their circle widened, and with the help of wind chimes, simple yet effective, whose beautiful music led them to their water trough, feed trough and barn. Their gentle melodies guided them through an unfamiliar world and became a symbol of hope and guidance. They were home now, in a place of love and care forever.

Slowly but surely, Frederick and Richard began to find their footing as they bumped into every square inch of the fence. Their two-acre pasture became their kingdom, a testament to the power of perseverance. As they explored their new home, the two large British cows, Maggie and Penny stepped up to provide motherly care for them. The big cows play with Richard and Frederick, and you can often find them chasing one another or head butting, trying to push each other backward. Even if one of the girls is playing with Frederick, who is smaller with neurological issues, the girls will let Frederick win by allowing him to push them backwards. Both boys have a "sweet tooth" and love oatmeal cookies. When Richard smells the cookies, he comes running and will take the cookie right out of your hand. However, you must help Frederick, who is 100% blind, and put the cookie into his waiting deformed mouth. Such a lovely and special time spent with the boys, and they are "rock stars" with all visitors. Moments like these are truly precious. Thank you, sweet Jesus.

Their story is a living example of God's unwavering love and care for all His creation. It is a reminder that even in the face of adversity, hope and compassion can prevail.

REFLECTION

Let us reflect on the lives of Frederick and Richard, two extraordinary animals who have taught us the true meaning of resilience and faith. May their story inspire us to embrace compassion and extend a helping hand to those in need.

PRAYER

Heavenly Father, let us pray for the continued well-being of these gentle souls and for the strength of those who care for them. May their story be a beacon of hope, illuminating the path for all who encounter it. In Jesus' name. Amen

"For I was hungry, and you fed me; I was thirsty, and you gave me a drink; I was a stranger, and you invited me into your home; I was naked, and you gave me clothing. I was sick, and you cared for me; I was in prison, and you visited me."

— MATTHEW 25:35-36

Richard and Frederick

THE SHEEP
OLIVE AND WINTER: A TALE OF REDEMPTION

"The Lord is my shepherd; I have all that I need."

— PSALM 23:1

WHEN THE WORLD as they knew it shifted and changed, with a new housing development threatening their peaceful existence, a flock of gentle sheep were facing an unknown and frightening world. Neighbors who lived near the property being sold understood the plight of these beautiful souls and wanted to help find them a loving, forever home. Moved by a profound sense of compassion, these caring neighbors rallied to rescue Olive and two other precious sheep as if their hearts were ignited by a divine spark. Like the Good Samaritan in Luke 10:25-37, they saw not just animals in need but souls yearning for safety and love. Sometimes, in the darkest hour, a beacon of hope emerges along with the very best of the human heart to result in kindness and compassion beyond measure.

Butterfly Field Farm was discovered via the Internet,

Tara and Ted were contacted, and the sanctuary opened its gates to welcome the three displaced sheep to their new home. Among them was Olive, a remarkable ewe whose gentle spirit was as vast as the open fields. She possessed an uncanny connection with humans, her gaze unwavering and trusting, a testament to the innate goodness that resides within all creatures. When Olive arrived, she was quite fluffy with white winter hair, or so Tara and Ted thought. Olive is a sheep that has hair instead of wool from the Katahdin breed. Soon, a surprise came, totally unexpected. On the first day of winter, the temperature dipped to a bone-chilling nineteen degrees. When Ted was doing the morning chores, he heard a "baby" crying in the back pasture. Upon closer inspection, he discovered a little, dry white ball of fluff next to Olive. She had given birth overnight in the harshest conditions, and they didn't even realize she was pregnant. Hence, the baby lamb's name had to be "Winter."

Olive, with a maternal instinct as profound as the love of God, nurtured her lamb with a tenderness that echoed the compassion of the shepherd in Psalm 23. She shielded him from the icy winds, her warmth a beacon in the frozen landscape. Winter thrived under her care, a testament to the enduring power of a mother's love. Just as the Lord watches over His flock Psalm 23:1, Olive watched over her lamb, her heart filled with a protective love that mirrored the divine.

Winter grew under Olive's watchful eye, not just in size but in spirit. Tall and proud, he became a protector of the flock, a symbol of redemption, rising from the fragility of newborn life to become a guardian. One of the most special qualities about Winter is his fearlessness. Daily, the sheep and donkeys are given treats in the pasture, and everyone dives in. The donkeys are much bigger, so all the sheep are very careful because the donkeys could become aggressive and kick. Only one sheep dares to dive into the middle of the madness, and that is baby Winter. Having grown up with the donkeys, he doesn't fear them but simply barrels into the middle of the herd, not concerned at all. The other sheep will nibble around the periphery of this mayhem while big boy Winter is firmly in the center. Gentle, sweet and forgiving, Winter is a wonderful example of grace in the fields. Just as the Israelites were once wandering and lost but found redemption through God's love, Winter had a perilous beginning out in a field one cold morning but soon found a home and purpose. His journey mirrored a life redeemed by grace.

In the peaceful sanctuary of Butterfly Field Farm, Olive and Winter are touching examples of kindness, love and hope that brings joy to everyone that they meet. We are reminded of the profound responsibility to care for all God's creatures. We are called to be channels of His love, extending compassion and kindness to all.

"Be kind to each other tenderhearted, forgiving each other just as Christ has forgiven you."

— EPHESIANS 4:32

REFLECTION

Let us be inspired and reflect on the unwavering love of Olive, the resilience of Winter, and the compassion of those who rescued them. Let us open our hearts and homes to those in need, mirroring the unconditional love of our Creator, God Almighty. Let us be instruments of His grace, extending a helping hand to the lost and forgotten, just as He seeks out the one lost sheep.

PRAYER

Lord, thank you for the beautiful example of Olive and Winter. May their story ignite in our hearts a flame of compassion for all your creatures. Grant us the courage to be your hands and feet, offering shelter, food and love to those in need. In Jesus' name, we pray. Amen

Olive and Winter

THE GOATS
MAVERICK AND GOOSE: A TESTAMENT TO REDEMPTION

"Be kind to each other, tenderhearted, forgiving one another, even as God through Christ has forgiven you." Ephesians 4:32

IN THE HEART OF CONNECTICUT, a tale of neglect and suffering unfolded amidst opulence. Over one hundred goats endured a life of deprivation under the care of a troubled soul. Their once vibrant spirits were dulled by neglect, their bodies bearing the scars of inadequate care. Like lost sheep wandering aimlessly, they lived in a world devoid of compassion. The story of Maverick and Goose is a poignant reflection of God's boundless grace and the transformative power of God's love to heal the broken in spirit.

Scripture tells us:

"The Lord is close to the brokenhearted and rescues those whose spirits are crushed."

— PSALM 34:18

These creatures, once brimming with life, were broken in spirit and body. Their world was a desolate wasteland, a far cry from the verdant fields promised in the Psalms.

Enslaved in a world of neglect and cruelty, Maverick and Goose were among the goats confined to a property steeped in darkness. Many were confined to the house and never saw outside. Their owner, a captive of mental illness, was unable to provide the care these innocent creatures deserved. A house of horrors it was. The police, agents of justice, were compelled to intervene, rescuing many from the brink of death. Yet, the cycle of suffering persisted as the resilient goats multiplied.

As the goats continued to grow constantly, a crisis point was reached. The goats, both inside and outside the home, were shadows of their potential. Emaciated and terrified, they were mere echoes of the creatures God intended them to be. Their owner, a prisoner of her own despair, faced the consequences of her actions, charged with a multitude of counts of cruelty. Many innocent lives were lost, a heartbreaking testament to the depths of human neglect.

Amidst this tragedy, a flicker of hope emerged. Healthy goats, survivors of this ordeal, were entrusted to the care of sanctuaries along the East Coast. Among them were Maverick and Goose, two spirits yearning for redemption. But the Lord is a tender Shepherd, and His love knows no bounds. Just as He gathers His flock, the gentle farmers at Butterfly Field Farm welcomed Maverick and Goose with open arms. Slowly, with unwavering patience, they nurtured the wounded spirits of these two precious creatures. It was as though they were tending to lost souls, offering hope where despair once reigned.

"Come to me, all of you that are weary and carry heavy burdens, and I will give you rest."

— MATTHEW 11:28

With each passing day, Maverick and Goose began to trust, their hearts slowly thawing under the warmth of human kindness. It was a testament to the power of love, a love that mirrors the boundless compassion of our Heavenly Father.

Their transformation was nothing short of miraculous. The once fearful creatures blossomed into affectionate companions, their spirits restored. Like the prodigal son returning home, they found acceptance, love, and a sense of belonging.

Their story is a powerful reminder of the redemptive power of love. It is a testament to the belief that even in the darkest of places, hope can flourish. Maverick and Goose, once victims of cruelty, became symbols of resilience, a living embodiment of God's grace.

As days turned into weeks and weeks into months, the icy walls of fear began to crumble. Their spirits, once broken, were mended through the tender care of their human guardians. Maverick and Goose, once symbols of despair, became beacons of hope. Their magnificent horns resemble wings about to take flight and are a breathtaking reminder of God's artistry. Both Maverick and Goose are now trusting humans and have become big snuggle bunnies.

Their journey mirrors the biblical narrative of redemption. Like the prodigal son, they returned from a life of hardship to find a loving embrace. Their story is a testament to the unwavering love of a compassionate God who restores and heals.

REFLECTION

Their story is a powerful reminder of the redemptive power of love. It is a testament to the belief that even in the darkest of places, hope can flourish. Maverick and Goose, once victims of cruelty, became symbols of resilience, a living embodiment of God's grace.

As we reflect on their journey, let us be inspired to extend compassion to all creatures, great and small. Let us strive to be instruments of God's love, offering hope and healing to those in need. And let us remember the words of the psalmist:

"The Lord is good to everyone. He shows compassion to all his creation."

— PSALM 145:9

PRAYER

O Lord, we pray for strength to be like the gentle farmers at Butterfly Field Farm, offering refuge and love to those who have lost their way. May we be a beacon of hope in a world that often seems shrouded in darkness. And may we always remember that even the most wounded souls can find redemption through the power of love and the grace of God. In Jesus' name. Amen

"For the Lord is good. His unfailing love continues forever, and his faithfulness continues to each generation."

— PSALM 100:5

Maverick and Goose

THE DONKEYS, SUSIE AND GERRY,

A RESCUED STORY OF FAITH AND COMPASSION

SUSIE AND GERRY, the first donkeys to arrive at Butterfly Field Farm, were rescued from the depths of despair. Rescued from a kill pen in Asheville, North Carolina, their story is a stark reminder of the horrific conditions equines endure in these facilities. These innocent creatures, devoid of owners, are condemned to a week-long torture before facing an unimaginable fate: slaughter and export for human consumption. The chaos, deprivation, and terror they experience are almost beyond comprehension.

Ted's heart was shattered as he witnessed this cruelty through a Facebook group. Among the suffering, he saw two donkeys destined for a brighter future. Their names, Susie and Gerry, held a profound resonance for Tara. A divine connection was undeniable as they shared names with Tara's mother (Susie) and her grandmother (Gerry). It was a clear call to action, a mandate from above to bring these precious souls to Butterfly Field Farm.

Six-year-old Susie, with her soulful grey eyes and her soft brown coat and her six-month-old son, Gerry, arrived timid and traumatized. Yet, amidst their fear, a gentle spirit shone through. Susie's immediate trust in Ted and Gerry's following in her footsteps were signs of hope. Their love for affection and human touch was a stark contrast to the horrors they had endured. Favorites with visitors, these gentle, loving animals found grace and peace in the fields of Butterfly Field Farm. They love the comforting caress of a brush and bask in the warmth of a gentle touch.

Ted and Tara, novices in donkey care, found themselves captivated by these gentle creatures. But their connection ran deeper than mere coincidence. The donkey, a symbol of humility and service in Scripture, holds a special place in Christian tradition. Matthew 21:5 tells of Jesus entering Jerusalem on a donkey, fulfilling prophecy and demonstrating His meekness.

The donkey's physical attributes also carry profound significance. The distinctive cross-like marking on its back is a testament to its enduring connection to the crucifixion of Jesus. Legend speaks of a colt, never ridden by anyone, called the Jerusalem donkey that carried Jesus into Jerusalem on Palm Sunday and accompanied Jesus to Calvary. A loyal companion who witnessed Jesus' suffering on the cross. In a beautiful act of love, the donkey refused to leave Jesus until the final moments, at which time he could no longer bear to look and turned his back on the cross in tears. The Lord imprinted the image of the cross upon its back, a symbol passed down through generations as a mark of honor from our Lord. True to this legend, Gerry has a thick dark brown line of fur that runs along the spine, intersected by another dark stripe across the shoulders, forming the shape of a cross. Susie's is the same but lighter and more distinctive.

REFLECTION

This story of rescue, redemption, and divine providence calls us to reflect on our role in the world. We are called to be compassionate stewards of all creation, to protect the vulnerable, and to embody the love and mercy of Christ. Just as Ted and Tara answered the call to rescue Susie and Gerry, we, too, are called to respond to the suffering around us.

PRAYER

Heavenly Father, we thank You for the compassion shown to Susie and Gerry. May their story inspire us to be channels of Your love and mercy. Grant us the courage to stand up for the voiceless and to work tirelessly for a world where all creatures are treated with kindness and respect. In Jesus' name, we pray. Amen

Susie & Gerry

THE STORY
OF PRINCESS LAMY:
A TALE OF REDEMPTION AND GRACE

"Acknowledge that the Lord is good! He made us, and we are his. We are his people, the sheep of his pasture." Psalm 100:3

IN THE PEACEFUL valley below the Blue Ridge Mountains, where the air was fresh, and the fields glowed with the early morning sun, an urgent call woke Ted and Tara from their slumber. At a nearby farm, one of the pregnant sheep began giving birth weeks ahead of schedule. Among the three newborns, one little lamb had been rejected by her mother. Faced with the heartbreaking reality that leaving her behind would lead to certain death, Ted and Tara, after consulting with the farm owner, decided to bring the rejected lamb home. Sadly, rejected baby lambs are called "bummer lambs," but soon, this little girl was going to be loved beyond comprehension.

That morning, it seemed as though Heaven's doors opened wide, and God touched Ted and Tara's hearts. With compassion and love, they chose to adopt the fragile lamb, naming her Princess Lamy. Wrapped in warmth and grace, they bottle-fed and cared for her as their own, knowing that God had entrusted them with her life. Ted took on the role of Lamy's mother. He bottle-fed her every two hours throughout the day and night. Princess Lamy slept beside Ted at night in tiny diapers and was given all the love his wonderful heart could give. Soon, Princess Lamy became part of the family. She wandered freely through the house, making herself at home on the couch, in the bed, and even playing with the family's four dogs. Her curious spirit led her to unravel rolls of toilet paper and explore every corner of her new world.

When she was strong enough, Lamy was introduced to the barnyard, where she met Baby Bo, another lamb in need of companionship, as he, too, was rejected by his mother. The two became inseparable, exploring the fields together and discovering the best patches of grass and clover. Though Lamy's own mother had rejected her, God had a greater plan. Her siblings were sent to market, but Lamy was spared, living a life of freedom, joy, and love under the watchful care of Ted and Tara and, ultimately, God. Even when she became a full-grown sheep out in the field with the rest of the flock, whenever she saw Ted or heard his voice, she came running no matter where she was. They have a bond that cannot be broken. Unconditional love is like the love our sweet Jesus feels for us.

REFLECTION

Princess Lamy's story is a beautiful reflection of God's redemptive love. Like Lamy, we are sometimes rejected, abandoned, or cast aside, but God, in His infinite grace, never leaves us. Just as Ted and Tara saved Lamy and gave her a new life, God rescues us from despair and hopelessness, giving us a life filled with hope and purpose. His love for us is deep, personal, and unconditional, always guiding us toward a better future, even when we can't see it ourselves.

"Even if my father and mother abandoned me, the Lord will hold me close."

— PSALM 27:10

"For I know the plans I have for you," says the Lord.

"They are plans for good and not for disaster, to give you a future and a hope."

— JEREMIAH 29:11

PRAYER

Heavenly Father, thank You for Your redeeming love that seeks us when we feel lost and forgotten. Thank You for the gift of compassion and for showing us, through stories like Lamy's, that Your grace is always present. Help us to trust in Your plans for our lives, even when we face rejection or uncertainty. May we always remember that You are our loving shepherd, guiding and protecting us. In Jesus' name. Amen.

Princess Lamy

BROWNIE, THE DONKEY WHO REFUSED TO QUIT:
A TALE OF REDEMPTION

"Sing a song to the Lord; praise his name! Each day proclaim the good news that he saves."

— PSALM 90:2

IN THE PEACEFUL pastures of Butterfly Field Farm, God was about to reveal His miraculous plan of redemption. A dear friend of Tara and Ted, recovering from a serious surgery, asked them to foster her two donkeys, Henry and Brownie, while she healed. As lovers of donkeys, Tara and Ted couldn't pass up the opportunity to care for these gentle creatures, especially since both had been rescued from a kill pen. Little did they know God was about to showcase His power through one of these donkeys.

Henry adjusted quickly, making friends with the other animals, but Brownie, the taller and younger of the two, went directly to a corner in the shelter and barely moved. For two days, Brownie stood still, not eating, drinking, or interacting with the others. His condition quickly declined,

24

and an emergency vet visit revealed he had severe pneumonia with the possibility of free fluid in his chest along with a scary high fever—a critical and often fatal condition.

"But God is so rich in mercy, and he loves us so much, even when we were dead because of our sins, he gave us life when he raised Christ from the dead."

— EPHESIANS 2:4

No doubt Brownie contracted the sickness at the kill pen. Very little concern is given to equines in these facilities. They receive enough food and water to stay alive but no vet care and bare minimum treatment in these horrible conditions. At Butterfly Field Farm, everything possible was being done to help Brownie, but he was scarcely responding to the medications. The fever remained awfully high at 104°F, and every attempt was being made to get it into the normal range of 97-100°F. He was barely eating and drinking. Tough conversations about the possibility of having to let him go began with the owner.

Just when hope seemed lost, God sent help. A friend's wife, a retired veterinarian, heard about the struggles he was having and joined the fight to help. She arrived and immediately began treating Brownie. His body was weak, his head hung low, and time was running out. Yet, God had other plans.

With careful attention, medication, and love, Brownie began to show small signs of life. Slowly but surely, he started eating, drinking and walking around. More vet professionals wanted to help join the cause and visited the farm with portable X-Ray equipment to take pictures of

Brownie's lungs. The resulting diagnosis confirmed severe pneumonia but no free fluid – an answer to prayer. We were blessed that many good, kind people were donating time and resources to help save this precious boy.

"I will give you back your health and heal you of your wounds, says the Lord."

— JEREMIAH 30:17

The healing continued as the once-fragile donkey gained weight and strength, and soon Brownie was back to running around the pasture, chasing goats with newfound energy. He had come back from the brink of death—living proof of God's grace and mercy.

After a follow-up exam with a mobile vet, it was confirmed that while there was still some infection in his lungs, Brownie's condition had drastically improved.

"The Lord nurses them when they are sick and restores them to health."

— PSALM 41:3

With more antibiotics, regular care, and much love, Brownie was finally well enough to return to his owner. His journey was nothing short of miraculous, a story of life restored and a testament to God's redemption.

REFLECTION

Brownie's story reminds us that God's love and healing power extend beyond human understanding. When we think all hope is lost, God is working behind the scenes, bringing life where there seems to be none. Just as He restored Brownie, God can bring healing and redemption to our lives, no matter how dire the situation. " Give thanks to the Lord of Heaven's Armies, for the Lord is good. His faithful love endures forever!" Jeremiah 33:10.

May we remember the goodness of the human heart to want to help in times of trouble. How grateful we are that so many wonderful people stepped up to help. We will never forget their kindness and sincere concern.

PRAYER

Dear Heavenly Father, we praise You for Your incredible love and mercy for restoring life when all seems lost. Thank You for the reminder that You are the Great Healer, Jehovah Rapha, capable of miracles far beyond our comprehension. Just as You breathed new life into Brownie, we ask that You breathe life into our hearts and our situations. Help us to trust in Your timing and never give up, knowing that You are always at work for our good. In Jesus' name. Amen

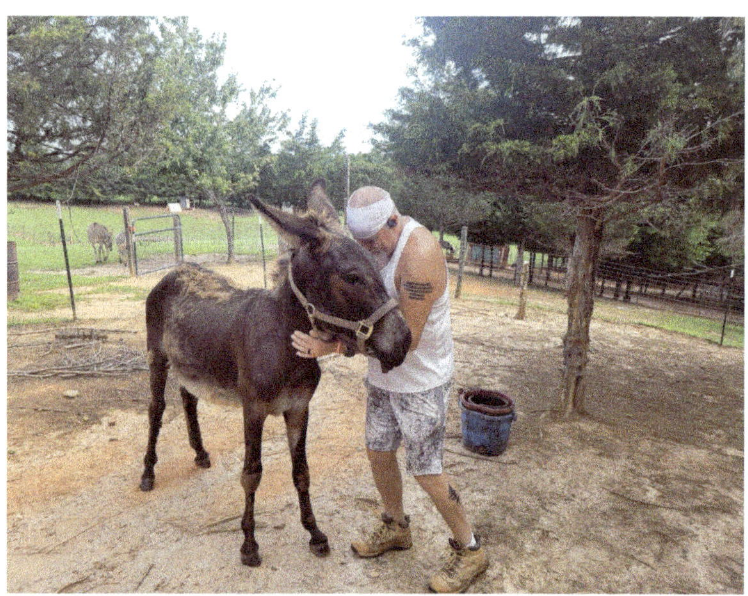

Brownie & Ted

TOM'S JOURNEY TO REDEMPTION:
A STORY OF GRACE AND MERCY

"Take delight in the Lord, and he will give you your hearts' desires."

— PSALM 37:4

ON THE WINDING, often treacherous narrow roads of the Blue Ridge Mountains, a truck carrying domesticated turkeys to a slaughterhouse for Thanksgiving overturned. Many of the birds did not survive, and several escaped into the woods. Among the survivors was Tom, a very large, gentle turkey with an injured foot.

Tom's journey from near death to recovery began when Animal Control rescued him and several others, bringing three turkeys to Butterfly Field Farm Animal Sanctuary—a place of healing and redemption. Here, animals are not just cared for physically but are given a chance to experience grace, love, and recovery, much like the redemption we receive through Christ.

When Tom arrived, he was not only injured but severely

overweight because these turkeys were purposely pumped with hormones to make them gain weight quickly to produce as much meat as possible. All for the sake of maximizing profits for the meat company. Tom arrived with two other turkeys who unfortunately did not survive. Despite his intimidating size—he weighed nearly 50 pounds—Tom had a heart full of gentleness. He was now in a place where he could heal, much like when the Lord watches over us in our times of need.

"The Lord is close to the brokenhearted; he rescues those whose spirits are crushed."

— PSALM 34:18

Tom received tender care from the caregivers at the sanctuary. His diet was adjusted, and he was given medicine to restore his health. Every evening, when Tara and Ted go to the barn to put away the animals, it is precious to watch Tara walk with Tom with her hand on his back, guiding him into the barn for the night. She gently talks to him all the way and helps when he stumbles. God smiles down on Tara and Ted as they care for His animals with love and kindness.

Although his foot was injured from the accident, it did not stop Tom from finding joy. His affectionate nature won over the hearts of everyone at the sanctuary, where he loved to have his head rubbed and gobbles happily when people gobble to him. What is so fascinating about turkeys is their amazing appearance. Their blue head feels soft and flesh-like, and they love to have their head rubbed if they are tame. The snood is a red, floppy, fleshy appendage that drapes over the turkey's beak. Its purpose is to attract mates, heat dissipation, indicator of health and mood indicator. The waddle is a flap of skin hanging under the chin connecting the throat and head and is red. Its purpose is basically the same as the snood, but it also indicates fear by changing color. Male turkeys also have what is called a beard found on their chest. This is a black tuft of modified feathers that starts growing shortly after they hatch but never fall off. Turkeys are truly an intricate creation with a beautiful display of feathers with a majestic array of tail feathers. Truly one of God's most beautiful and incredible creations.

Tom's resilience and gentle spirit remind us of the promise in Isaiah 40:31

"But those who trust in the Lord will find new strength. They will soar high on wings like eagles. They will run and not grow weary, they will walk and not faint."

REFLECTION

Tom's presence became a symbol of God's mercy and care, reflecting the truth that even when we are broken, God never abandons us. Like Tom, who delights in chasing two beautiful white turkey hens around in the barnyard despite his physical limitations, we too can find purpose and joy despite our own brokenness. For it is through His grace that we are healed and made whole.

Tom's story, like ours, is a testimony of redemption, reminding us that no matter how far we may fall or how broken we may feel, God's grace is sufficient to restore and redeem us.

"God saved you by His grace when you believed. And you can't take credit for this, it is a gift from God."

— EPHESIANS 2:8

PRAYER

Heavenly Father, thank You for the grace and mercy that You pour over all of creation, from the animals in our care to the people who seek Your love. Help us to recognize that, like Tom, we are all broken in some way, but find our healing and redemption in You. May we always extend Your kindness to every living thing, reflecting Your love and compassion. In Jesus' name. Amen

Beautiful Tom the Turkey

EMBER ROSE AND MAGGIE:
A STORY OF LOVE AND HOPE

"I take joy in doing Your will, my God, for Your instructions are written on my heart."

— PSALM 40:8

WHEN THE SANCTUARY was first started, mini cows weren't part of the plan, but their undeniable charm always caught our eye. So, when a dear friend and fellow sanctuary founder called needing help, we were quick to say yes. Her sanctuary was temporarily closing so she could care for her sick daughter, and she needed us to take in two of her mini animals: a little donkey named Eeyore and a mini cow named Ember Rose.

When they arrived, we kept Ember Rose and Eeyore together in the barnyard. However, it wasn't long before Ember Rose showed interest in the other cows. We decided to move her into the cow pasture, keeping a close watch. Amazingly, the cows immediately accepted her, treating her as if she were one of their own calves.

I called our friend to share the update, and she revealed something I hadn't known—Ember Rose had never known her mother. As if by divine design, one of our British White Cows, Maggie, stepped in, mothering Ember as if she were her own, even letting her nurse despite not having milk. Maggie's nurturing care gave Ember the sense of love and safety she had never experienced.

As time passed, Ember Rose blossomed. She could often be seen running joyfully across the pasture, free at last to embrace her true self. At first, she was very shy, pulling away when someone tried to pet her. But that changed when we started carrying her favorite treats in our pocket. Soon enough, she began to trust us, running to greet us every day, knowing we always had a treat and a warm embrace waiting for her. Ember Rose now allows us to love on her as long as we want, and her bond with Maggie remains strong. They are always side by side in the pasture—an unexpected family, but a family nonetheless.

REFLECTION

The way Maggie adopted Ember Rose, providing love and care despite not being her mother, reminds me of God's love for all His creatures. In Psalm 36:6, it is written:

> "You care for people and animals alike, O Lord. How precious is Your unfailing love, O God!"

Just as God watches over all of His creation, we are called to care for the animals entrusted to us. His love for all living things is a model for the compassion we show in our sanctuary.

Ember's story is also a testament to the hope and restoration God offers. In Isaiah 11:6, we read about the peaceable kingdom where:

"On that day, the wolf and the lamb will live together, and the leopard will lie down with the baby goat. The calf and yearling will be safe with the lion, and the little child will lead them all. The cow will graze near the bear. The cub and the calf will lie down together. The lion will eat hay like the cow."

This passage speaks of harmony, which is what we strive to foster here at Butterfly Field—an environment where every animal can find safety, love, and a new beginning.

REFLECTION

Ember Rose never knew her mother, but by God's design, she was mothered by Maggie. A reminder that love transforms all. Whether it's an animal or a person, when we are cared for, we thrive. God calls us to be stewards of His creation, to provide safe havens for the vulnerable, and to nurture life in all its forms.

~

PRAYER

Let us pray: Heavenly Father, thank You for the gift of animals and the beauty they bring into our lives. Help us to reflect Your love by caring for them with compassion and kindness. Just as Maggie embraced Ember Rose, may we also embrace those who need care, whether human or animal. Guide us to be faithful stewards of Your creation, always mindful of the responsibility You've given us. In the precious name of Jesus, we pray. Amen

Ember Rose & Maggie

LITTLE MAN YAZ'S JOURNEY:
A STORY OF LOVE, HOPE, AND NEW BEGINNINGS

"This means that anyone who belongs to Christ has become a new person. The old life is gone, the new life has begun!"

— **2 CORINTHIANS 5:17**

LAST SUMMER, Butterfly Field Farm welcomed Yaz, a beautiful miniature horse, into its sanctuary. It was more than just a new home; it was a place of refuge, much like the refuge God provides for all His creatures.

"The Lord is good to everyone; He showers compassion on all His creation."

— PSALM 145:9

Yaz's first year at the farm was quite the adventure, but every moment reflected God's hand of protection and love. Yaz was being advertised on Craig's List when his story began with a concerned call from our friends at Onyx's Dream, a local animal rescue. They had saved Yaz's half-brother and were deeply worried about the conditions Yaz was living in. In that moment, God's providence shone through when a kindhearted sponsor stepped forward, covering Yaz's adoption fees. Diane Collins even traveled with us to bring Yaz home from his place of neglect into the loving arms of Butterfly Field Farm. Yaz was so tiny that he fit comfortably in the back of an SUV! Diane sponsors Yaz and calls him her own as she visits regularly, providing food and lots and lots of hugs and kisses as she gently brushes him.

"God sets the lonely in families."

— PSALM 68:6

And on that wonderful day, Yaz found his family at Butterfly Field Farm.

Upon arrival, Yaz longed to be close to the bonded pair of miniature horses, Yin and Yang. But they weren't ready to welcome him just yet. Instead of giving up, Yaz learned to stay close enough to feel their presence while respecting their boundaries, patiently waiting for his time to be embraced. His resilience and determination reflect the truth in Galatians 6:9,

"So let's not get tired of doing good. At just the right time, we will reap a harvest of blessings if we don't give up."

Yaz also had a bit of a mischievous streak, testing his

boundaries as young animals often do. But after he was neutered, something changed. He became calmer and less aggressive - it was then that Yin and Yang finally accepted him into their little herd. Now, the three are inseparable, moving as one. When relocating them to new pastures, only one lead rope is needed on Yin and Yang—Yaz faithfully follows, trusting and secure in their companionship.

In this story, we see a reflection of God's promise to make all things new.

"Those who live in the shelter of the Most High will find rest in the shadow of the Almighty."

— PSALM 91:4

At Butterfly Field Farm, Yaz has not only found safety but also the love of a new family. He continues to grow, not just in size but in spirit, becoming a favorite among the farm's visitors, a living testament to God's compassionate care.

REFLECTION

Yaz's journey reminds us that God cares for every living thing. He rescues, restores, and provides a home for the vulnerable and lost. Just as Yaz found refuge and love at Butterfly Field Farm, we are reminded that God's love is boundless, extending to all of creation. In His care, both people and animals find peace, safety, and renewal.

~

PRAYER

Heavenly Father, we thank You for the way You watch over Your creation, big and small. Thank You for bringing Yaz into the safety of Butterfly Field Farm and for the love and care he now receives. Help us to be instruments of Your love and compassion, to care for the animals and the world You have entrusted to us. May we reflect Your grace and mercy in all that we do. In Jesus' name. Amen

Gentle Yaz

MRS. POTTS:
A STORY OF REDEMPTION AND GRACE

"God saved you by His grace when you believed. And you can't take credit for this. It is a gift from God."

— EPHESIANS 2:8

MRS. POTTS, our beloved senior donkey at Butterfly Field Farm, spent most of her life roaming free as a wild burro in the California deserts. Like so many of God's creatures, she lived with the simple joys of creation—carefree and untamed.

"The earth is the Lord's, and everything in it."

— PSALM 24:1

And Mrs. Potts was part of that divine freedom, thriving in her natural habitat.

However, each year, the Bureau of Land Management

rounds up these majestic animals to find homes for them. It was then that Mrs. Potts' life changed, but God's hand was upon her, guiding her path.

"The Lord protects all those who love Him."

— PSALM 145:20

And she was one of the fortunate ones rescued by Peaceful Valley Donkey Rescue, a beacon of grace and kindness. She was brought to Virginia, where she would find not only a new home but a new purpose.

Mrs. Potts later came to Butterfly Field Farm and instantly became a surrogate mother to a young donkey named Chip. Everywhere Mrs. Potts went, he followed. Always wanting to be near her. Unfortunately, Chip passed away on November 19, 2020, from heart disease shortly after Mrs. Potts arrived. Her role as a mother figure was cut short, but her presence remained a blessing to the other donkeys.

"He heals the brokenhearted and bandages their wounds."

— PSALM 147:3

Mrs. Potts, with her quiet strength, became a source of comfort to us all, especially her herd.

At 31 years old, Mrs. Potts is the farm's oldest female donkey and has taken on the role of matriarch. Twice a day, she and her fellow senior donkeys, Jasper and Frankie, gather in the small feeding area to receive their senior feed. Winter is approaching, and just as the Lord prepares the earth for new seasons, so too are we caring for these gentle souls, providing for them as:

"for the Lord is good to all; He has compassion on all his creation."

— PSALM 145:9

During feeding time, Mrs. Potts always eats beside Jasper, keeping her hindquarters firmly against him—her way of making sure he knows not to steal her food! But there's a playful spirit between them, like children teasing one another. If Jasper finishes his meal first, Mrs. Potts will graciously share hers, reflecting the kindness that flows from a heart of love. And they both show deep respect for Frankie, who is allowed to eat in peace.

"Be kind and compassionate to one another, tender-hearted, forgiving one another, just as God through Christ has forgiven you."

— EPHESIANS 4:32

And indeed, these donkeys embody that simple, powerful truth.

Though Mrs. Potts was a little testy when she first arrived, she has found peace within her herd. On her first visit with the farrier, she needed to be sedated to relax as she did not like getting her hooves trimmed. But now she is a champion, stands very still and lets the farrier gently clip and shape her hooves. As a reward, she gets lots of treats to keep her occupied during this time. She settled into her new life as a redeemed and cared-for creature, just as we are called to settle into God's loving arms when He brings us into His fold.

"The Lord is my shepherd; I have all that I need."

— PSALM 23:1

And Mrs. Potts, through the grace of God and the love she receives here, lacks nothing in her golden years.

REFLECTION

Mrs. Potts' journey from a wild burro to a cherished member of our sanctuary is a beautiful reminder of God's redemptive love for all His creation. Just as He provided for Mrs. Potts and brought her into a safe, loving home, God cares for each one of us. No matter our past, He prepares a place for us where we can find rest, provision, and peace.

❧

PRAYER

Heavenly Father, we thank You for the gift of life and the way You care for all Your creatures, great and small. We are reminded through Mrs. Potts that Your love knows no bounds and that You are the great provider and healer. Help us to extend that same compassion and kindness to all living beings, stewarding Your creation with love. In the precious name of Jesus. Amen

Mrs. Potts

MAGGIE AND PENNY'S REDEMPTION:
A STORY OF LOVE AND NEW BEGINNINGS

"And do everything with love."

— 1 CORINTHIANS 16:14

IN THE PEACEFUL green pastures of Butterfly Field Farm, Maggie and Penny, two beautiful British White cows with black hooves, noses and ears, found a new life, a life of love and safety, far from the fate that once loomed over them. These herd sisters were born on a beef farm in Virginia, but thanks to the love of a farmer's daughter named Chay, their story took a very different turn. At just six months old, they were removed from the farm and placed in safe pastures, spared from the potential of slaughter.

But as life often goes, change comes. Chay's family needed to relocate from Virginia to Texas, and with a heavy heart, Chay desperately sought a new home for Maggie and Penny. Tearfully, she made a call to us at Butterfly Field Farm. Soon after, Maggie and Penny were safely settled at the farm, a bittersweet moment for Chay, yet she was comforted knowing her beloved cows had found a sanctuary where they would be loved forever. A forever home.

Now at Butterfly Field Farm, Maggie and Penny thrive and are popular with visitors because of their imposing size and gentle demeanor. Penny, the more outgoing of the two, is full of personality and loves nothing more than oatmeal cookies. She has no qualms about pushing others aside for treats, and despite her imposing 1,300-pound frame, her joyful spirit shines.

Maggie, on the other hand, is more reserved shy around humans, but her heart opened in a remarkable way when a mini-cow named Ember arrived at the farm. Though they are not related, and Maggie has no milk to offer, she allows Ember to nurse as a sign of comfort and love. They are often found resting side by side, a beautiful display of the maternal care Maggie has developed for Ember.

This bond illustrates the transformative power of love and redemption. Maggie and Penny, once bound for an uncertain future, have found sanctuary where their true selves are revealed, free to form connections not only with one another but with others around them.

"Dear Friends, let us continue to love one another, for love comes from God."

— 1 JOHN 4:7

"For all creation is waiting eagerly for that future day when God will reveal who His children really are."

— ROMANS 8:19

Just as creation eagerly awaits redemption, Maggie and Penny's story reflects God's hand in offering new life and hope to all creatures. In His plan, He cares for every living thing, giving them refuge and the opportunity to live in love and safety.

"What is the price of five sparrows-two copper coins? Yet God does not forget a single one of them."

— LUKE 12:6

If God remembers even the smallest creatures, how much more does He care for the ones, like Maggie and Penny, who have been saved from certain death and given a chance to live in the fullness of His care?

REFLECTION

Maggie and Penny's journey reminds us of the importance of compassion, not just for people but for all of God's creatures. When we extend love, even to animals, we participate in God's redemptive work in creation. The safe haven these cows have found is a reflection of the refuge God offers to all who seek Him.

PRAYER

Dear Lord, we thank You for the beauty of Your creation and the love You extend to every living being. We are grateful for the stories of animals like Maggie and Penny, who remind us of Your grace and the new life You provide. Help us to be stewards of Your creation, showing compassion and care to all creatures. Let us see Your hand at work in all of Your creatures, and may we be moved to protect and nurture them. In the loving name of Jesus, we pray. Amen

Penny and Maggie

ONE HORN JACK:
A STORY OF HOPE AND NEW LIFE

"For I know the plans I have for you, says the Lord. They are plans for good and not for disaster, to give you a future and a hope."

— JEREMIAH 29:11

JACK, a beautiful brown goat, came to Butterfly Field Farm with just one horn and an endearing nickname, "One Horn Jack." How he lost his horn, we do not know. Once destined for slaughter, Jack's future looked bleak. Yet, God's grace worked through kind neighbors, Sue and James, who saw beyond his fate. They noticed his gentle spirit, believing Jack had been raised as a pet, and felt called to intervene. Moved by compassion, they rescued Jack, bringing him to a place of love and new beginnings.

From the moment he arrived at the farm, it was clear that Jack carried a unique warmth, approaching every human with trust and friendship.

"A cheerful heart is good medicine, but a broken spirit saps a person's energy."

— PROVERBS 17:22

Jack quickly won the hearts of everyone on the farm, spreading joy to every visitor he met. And with his strikingly beautiful brown coat and single horn, he brought a rare and special charm that made him unforgettable.

Jack's presence became a source of comfort and happiness to the other residents as he shared his gentle companionship across many species. He joined a pasture with sheep, cows, and guardian donkeys—a mixed group with whom he felt at ease. His bond with the animals grew quickly, and he formed a special friendship with baby Winter, the lamb, as if he had found his place among them. Just as Psalm 36:6 tells us:

"You care for people and animals alike, O Lord. How precious is Your unfailing love, O God!"

God had gently placed Jack right where he was needed most.

Despite his past challenges, Jack's spirit stayed strong. Even grouchy Jasper, another senior donkey, couldn't intimidate him, as Jack learned to stand his ground with patience and respect. His resilience and gentleness reminded us of God's promise in Philippians 3:4-5,

"Always be full of joy in the Lord. I say it again-rejoice! Let everyone see that you are considerate in all you do."

Jack's life was no longer bound by his past; he had found a family, freedom, and a purpose.

When the time came to introduce Jack to the barnyard with the other goats, he led the way. Jack is large in stature, very stately and is a born leader. Jack showed us where he feels most at home, just as each of our residents communicates their needs. In our hearts, we trust that God's plan for each of them is perfect, aligning with Proverbs 12:10,

"The godly care for the needs of their animals."

And here at Butterfly Field Farm, we believe in honoring that care.

REFLECTION

Reflect on how you can show compassion in your own life, perhaps by helping a local shelter, adopting a rescue animal, or supporting animal sanctuaries like Butterfly Field. God's call to care for His creatures is an invitation to bring His love to the world in all forms. Let us be mindful stewards, opening our hearts to those who rely on us for hope and a new beginning.

PRAYER

Dear Lord, thank You for showing us Your compassion and grace through the animals You have delivered to us. Just as You saved Jack from his dark path, help us to bring light and love to all creatures, understanding that they, too, seek peace, safety, and belonging. Teach us to open our hearts to Your call for kindness, to rescue those in need, and to offer a place of love and healing. Guide us to honor every life, large or small, as a gift from You. In Jesus' name. Amen

One Horn Jack

CHARLIE:
A LOYAL COMPANION AND FAITHFUL FRIEND

"A real friend sticks closer than a brother."

— **PROVERBS 18:24**

CHARLIE MAY NOT BE a farm animal or a rescue, but she has been an essential part of Butterfly Field Farm Animal Sanctuary from the very beginning. Not long after Tara and Ted moved from Florida to Virginia, long before they dreamed of a sanctuary, they brought home a beautiful yellow American Labrador Retriever puppy. Faithful, gentle, and ever so loyal, Charlie quickly became a cherished part of their family.

Charlie's nature reminds us of the Scripture that says:

"A friend is always loyal, and a brother is born to help in time of need."

— PROVERBS 17:17

Just as Charlie's gentle spirit and loyalty have brought comfort and companionship, they see God's faithfulness through her, reminding us of His constant presence and care.

Through the years, Charlie has proven her worth in countless ways. She accompanies Tara and Ted daily as they go about their chores, moving easily among all the animals, from baby chicks to full-grown donkeys. She has been bumped, pecked, headbutted, and even driven into the fence by a protective sheep. Yet, like Christ, who forgave even as He was wounded.

"He was oppressed and treated harshly, yet He never said a word."

— ISAIAH 53:7

Charlie returns each morning with joy, excited to begin a new day together. Her enduring patience and willingness to help, even after hardships, reflect a beautiful spirit of obedience and forgiveness.

Though she is starting to slow down at 8 years of age, her faithfulness never wavers. In the last two years, she has had two grand mal seizures, but they were infrequent enough to prevent the vet from placing her on medication just yet. Tara and Ted never know when a seizure will happen, however, they are prepared to assist her by just being there calmly, talking her through it and making sure she is safe. Telling her she will be alright and being present just like our Heavenly Father helps us through our trials with His sweet love. Charlie brings joy to everyone, including sanctuary visitors, and her loyalty has been a blessing to us all. When they need help putting the animals away for the night, particularly the mischievous goats and wandering ducks, Charlie assists with obedience and understanding. She stays in position, knowing that her gentle guidance helps these animals find their way back to their home and safety—just as we trust in God's guidance for our own lives. As Psalm 32:8 reminds us:

> "I will instruct you and teach you in the way you should go; I will counsel you with my loving eye on you."

REFLECTION

Charlie's steadfast loyalty reminds us of how we are called to be faithful and obedient, not only in our relationship with others but in our walk with God. Just as Charlie trusts us to guide her, may we place our trust fully in our loving Creator. Let her loyalty inspire us to stay committed, even when the path is difficult.

PRAYER

Heavenly Father, thank You for the example of love and faithfulness we see in Charlie. May we learn from her trust, her loyalty, and her obedience. Help us to reflect these qualities in our own lives, following You with joy and steadfastness. Guide us as You guide all of Your creation. In Jesus' name. Amen

Charlie and Friends

THE PIGS

A CLOSER LOOK AT THESE INTELLIGENT
AND AFFECTIONATE ANIMALS

"But ask the animals, and they will teach you, or the birds in the sky, and they will tell you, or speak to the earth, and it will teach you, or let the fish in the sea inform you."

—JOB 12: 7

ONCE UPON A TIME, four little pigs named Pooh Bear, Wilbur, Rocky, and Creed found their way to Butterfly Field Farm. They arrived from a hoarding situation in Charlottesville, VA, where their previous owner, though well-meaning, struggled to care for them. The environment grew unsafe as breeding spiraled out of control, and the little pigs were soon in need of a stable, loving home. Thankfully, when another sanctuary reached out to help rescue these poor animals, Butterfly Field Farm also answered the call with open arms. Few realize that pigs are extremely prolific and can have upwards of 3 litters per year, each litter producing a dozen babies or more. Imagine one mother pig having almost 40 babies per year!! No wonder things got completely out of control.

Pooh Bear, black in color and curious, always approaches the fence first, sniffing for treats and greeting new friends. Wilbur, with his unique spotted coat, is quiet but sociable. These two boys are a Pot-Bellied mix breed, but their exact lineage is unknown. Rocky and Creed are brothers, each with a gentle spirit and an easy-going nature. These boys are also part Pot-Bellied pig but, in addition, contain Boar in their genetics as indicative of their elongated snouts and protruding tusks. In their pen they live in harmony, no one pig dominating the others, each one embodying a calm, comforting presence. Remarkably clean and orderly, however, they savor their mud baths, which helps to keep them cool in the hot summer months. Even though pigs love to wallow in the mud, when it comes to their bathroom habits, they are very picky. They keep the interior of their pen extremely clean and love when Ted throws in new straw to lay on. The pigs also keep their yard very clean and only use the bathroom at the very end of their property, up against the fence.

These pigs remind us of the redeeming grace God extends to all creatures, calling them into lives of safety, love, and companionship. Just as God provides a:

"home for the lonely"

— PSALM 68:6

He brought these four pigs to a safe haven where they could finally experience love, companionship, and security. Despite their challenging start, Pooh Bear, Wilbur, Rocky, and Creed are living proof that even in the most difficult of situations, God's hand is there, guiding and redeeming.

REFLECTION

The gentle nature of these pigs mirrors the verse, "The Lord is good to everyone. He showers compassion on all His creation." Psalm 145:9. Through His kindness, they have found peace and companionship in one another and a family at Butterfly Field Farm. Their journey encourages us to be kind and compassionate, opening our hearts to those in need, just as Tara and Ted did for them.

PRAYER

Heavenly Father, thank You for the example of love, companionship, and redemption found in these four little pigs that have now grown into four very large pigs weighing approximately 200 pounds each. Just as You provided them with a safe place, we ask for Your grace today to be vessels of Your love to others. Teach us to care deeply, to serve faithfully, and to provide refuge for those in need. May our actions reflect Your compassion as we seek to love every creature You've made. In Jesus' name. Amen

Wilbur, Pooh Bear, Rocky and Creed

NOAH

THE MISCHIEVOUS, JOYFUL LEADER OF THE LITTLES

"Let the heavens rejoice, let the earth be glad; let the sea resound, all that is in it."

— **PROVERBS 96:11**

AT BUTTERFLY FIELD FARM, every resident has a story and personality as unique as God's fingerprints on creation. Among them is Noah, a spirited Nigerian Dwarf goat whose charm and leadership light up the farm. Noah's story began at Peaceful Valley Donkey Rescue, located in Concord, VA, about 45 minutes from Bedford, where he and his twin sister, Hope, were born. Earlier Peaceful Valley had accepted a male goat they were told was fixed. Turns out he was not and impregnated 4 of the female goats. Overbreeding is a huge issue with farm animals and one of the main reasons sanctuaries like Butterfly Field Farm exist. Noah, Hope and their mother, Heather, came to Butterfly Field Farm when the baby goats were just five days old. Joining them was Jasmine, the herd sister of Heather who was also pregnant at the time. Hiro and Faith were born at the farm shortly after they arrived. Noah, Hope, Hiro and Faith were raised together as a very tight-knit group.

The Littles—Noah, Hope, Hiro, and Faith—have shared not only their joyous beginnings but also the sorrows of losing their mothers. Both Heather and Jasmine passed in 2023 at the age of 14. Yet through it all, they have found family in one another and joy in life, reminding us of Psalm 68:6,

"God sets the lonely in families."

Noah, with his mischievous charm and natural leadership, stands out among the Littles. His knack for finding trouble—like sneaking into places he shouldn't—often brings laughter to those who witness it. Even when he leads the Littles outside the fenced areas, his sweet demeanor makes it hard to be upset with him. At the sound of his name, Noah and his troupe scamper back, their antics a source of endless amusement. Noah embodies Proverbs 17:22,

"A cheerful heart is good medicine."

His playful nature and leadership bring smiles to everyone at the farm, demonstrating the joy God has woven into His creation. Animals like Noah remind us of the delight and care our Creator has for all His works, as Psalm 104:24 reflects:

"How many are Your works, Lord! In wisdom, You made them all; the earth is full of Your creatures."

Noah's story reminds us of God's intentional design in every creature. His leadership among the Littles mirrors the way we are called to lead with love and care. Noah's mischievous but endearing antics teach us to embrace joy and laughter as gifts from God, even in the midst of daily responsibilities.

REFLECTION

Through Noah and the Littles, we see God's love and creativity on display. These animals not only bring joy to our lives but also teach us about resilience, community, and the simple pleasures of God's creation.

PRAYER

Heavenly Father, thank You for the joy and laughter You bring into our lives through the animals You've created. Thank You for their unique personalities that remind us of Your creativity and love. Help us to care for them as stewards of Your creation and to cherish the happiness they bring. In the precious name of Jesus, we pray. Amen

Hiro, Hope, Faith and Noah

MILO AND OTIS:
A REDEMPTION STORY

"Great is his faithfulness; his mercies begin afresh each morning."

— LAMENTATIONS 3:22-23

MILO AND OTIS were among the first goats to find refuge at Butterfly Field Farm and remain the only Boer goats in the sanctuary's herd. Their journey began in despair, as they were discovered on an abandoned farm where the owner had moved away, leaving animals behind to fend for them-selves. The reasons for this tragedy remain unclear, but what is known is that Milo and Otis were found in a state of severe neglect. So emaciated that the rescuers at Peaceful Valley Donkey Rescue feared they would not survive.

Yet, God's plan for these two was far from over. As it says in Psalm 34:18,

"The Lord is close to the brokenhearted and saves those who are crushed in spirit."

Milo and Otis were given comfort, safety, and care, and they began to respond to the healing touch of veterinary treatment and the love of those who refused to give up on them. Slowly but surely, their frail bodies strengthened, and their spirits began to shine again.

By the time they arrived at Butterfly Field Farm, Milo and Otis were no longer teetering on the brink of death but had become symbols of resilience and redemption. Isaiah 61:3 reminds us of God's promise to bestow on us:

"A crown of beauty instead of ashes, the oil of joy instead of mourning, and a garment of praise instead of a spirit of despair."

These goats, once abandoned and hopeless, now live vibrant lives full of joy and purpose.

Otis has taken on the role of herd leader, confidently guiding the other animals and ensuring harmony within the group. Milo, equally spirited, enjoys interacting with visitors and volunteers, delighting in the affection and treats he receives. Together, they embody the truth of 2 Corinthians 5:17,

"If anyone is in Christ, a new creation has come: The old has gone, the new is here!"

Their past suffering is behind them, replaced with a life of love, care, and security.

At Butterfly Field Farm, Milo and Otis are a living testament to God's redeeming power, a reminder that He rescues and restores all who are lost and broken. They will never face abandonment or fear again, but instead, they will continue to live out their days in peace and plenty.

REFLECTION

How often do we feel abandoned or forgotten, weighed down by the trials of life? Milo and Otis remind us that God never leaves us in despair. Just as He provided a way for these two goats to be saved, He offers us redemption and new life through His love.

PRAYER

Heavenly Father,

We praise You for Your unfailing love and for the redemption You bring to all of creation. Thank You for rescuing Milo and Otis from the brink of death and giving them a new life full of love and care. Let their story remind us of Your promise to restore and renew us, no matter how broken we may feel. Help us to see the beauty in Your creation and to show compassion to those who are hurting. May we always be instruments of Your grace and redemption. In Jesus' name. Amen

Milo and Otis

FREDDY
A GENTLE SOUL OF BUTTERFLY FIELD FARM

"We may make our plans, but God has the last word."

— **PROVERBS 16:1**

FREDDY WAS a 30-year-old miniature donkey when he came to the sanctuary with his wife, Freda and daughter, Frankie. They came to Butterfly Field Farm by way of Peaceful Valley Donkey Sanctuary. While they had found a new family here, there was both joy and heartache along the way. Shortly after this family arrived, Freda became seriously ill with kidney disease and died. There was absolutely nothing Tara and Ted could do as she was bleeding internally. In the aftermath, they ran tests on Freddy and his daughter, Frankie, relieved to find both had healthy kidneys by God's grace.

During this experience, Tara and Ted observed how donkeys mourn their dead, just as we do. As Freda lay in the pasture waiting for kindred souls to arrive to remove her body, Frankie stood over her mother, silent and still, like a guardian protecting her family. After Freda's body was removed, Frankie brayed frequently for almost a month, day and night, crying out for her mother. Even Jesus wept at the loss of his dear friend Lazarus, as written in John 11:35,

"Jesus wept"

As time does, little by little, the braying lessened, but what an amazing realization to understand the deep emotion these beautiful animals feel. Animals do have feelings, even though some dispute that fact. Witnessing such love and devotion for one another reminds us of Christ's deep love for us, His children.

Freddy's past is a mystery, but a scar on his face suggests he might have experienced neglect. Yet, like so many of God's creatures, Freddy held no bitterness. Although shy at first, Freddy learned to trust again even seek out love from visitors. His kindness reminds us of God's amazing love and grace, reflecting the tenderness that remains even in a heart that has known hardship. Freddy's favorite part of the day was also Tara and Ted's. Each evening, he stayed alone in the barnyard, where he peacefully enjoyed his senior feed, free from the usual barnyard commotion. During this time, he always allowed Ted to brush and love on him, and those quiet moments felt like a gift—a reminder of the deep bond that can grow when we care for God's creatures with patience and love.

Freddy's gentleness calls to mind Proverbs 12:10, which reminds us:

"The righteous care for the needs of their animals…"

Even though animals cannot speak, their lives often mirror qualities like loyalty, resilience, and forgiveness, traits that can inspire us all. Freddy's story demonstrates how even a neglected animal can bloom into a gentle, loving companion when given care and compassion. He became a beacon of kindness and patience for everyone he met, showing the sanctuary's visitors that true gentleness and love can transcend past hurt.

Miniature donkeys like Freddy are special. Originating from the Mediterranean islands of Sicily and Sardinia, their small stature is a natural characteristic, standing no taller than 36 inches and weighing between 200 and 400 pounds. In many ways, Freddy reminds us of the gentleness God calls us to embody in our lives. As it says in James 3:17,

> "But the wisdom from above is first of all pure. It is also peace loving, gentle at all times, and willing to yield to others."

Freddy's gentle spirit speaks to the wisdom that comes with a life marked by resilience and quiet strength.

Unfortunately, Freddy passed away November 30, 2023. He was loved deeply and will be sorely missed. Rest in peace sweet little man, rest in peace.

REFLECTION

Freddy's story is a gentle reminder of how kindness and patience can bring healing, not only to animals but also to our hearts. How can we show God's love and care to those who need it, including the creatures that share our world?

PRAYER

Heavenly Father, thank You for the gentle creatures in our lives, like Freddy, who teach us so much about love, patience, and resilience. May we always remember to care for them as Your Word instructs. Help us to reflect Your gentleness and compassion in all we do, reaching out to both animals and people in need with kindness. In Jesus' name, we pray. Amen

Gentle Freddy

BUCKY'S
RESCUE AND REDEMPTION

"The godly care for their animals, but the wicked are always cruel."

— PROVERBS 12:10

BUCKY, a full-grown Nigerian Dwarf goat, carries a story of resilience and redemption that reflects God's boundless compassion for all His creation. Despite his small stature, likely a result of being the runt of his litter, Bucky's journey reveals the tender care of a Creator who never overlooks even the smallest of His creatures. Bucky is the cutest little guy with a pure black coat and came to Butterfly Field Farm at one year old. The farm has many obstacles upon which the goats can climb, including giant wooden electric wire spools donated to the farm from the electric company, along with tables and ramps. Often, you will see Bucky standing at the very top of one of these obstacles, almost like saying, "I'm the king of the world."

Bucky was found wandering the streets of Bedford

County, Virginia, lost and alone. Taken in by Animal Control, he was brought to the Bedford County Animal Shelter, where efforts were made to reunite him with his original family. However, no one came forward to claim him, and as time passed, Bucky remained unwanted, overlooked by potential adopters. Yet, in God's perfect timing, a new chapter was about to unfold for this little goat.

"There will be no mercy for those who have not shown mercy to others. But if you have been merciful, God will be merciful when he judges you."

— JAMES 2:12

Butterfly Field Farm, with its mission rooted in God's love for His animals, maintains a close relationship with the Bedford County Animal Shelter. When the shelter reached out to the farm to ask if Bucky could join the sanctuary, the answer was yes, absolutely. After a veterinary visit for neutering and a thorough health check, Bucky arrived at the farm, where he was welcomed with open arms and warm hearts. Slowly but surely, he began to integrate into the goat herd, forming bonds and finding his place in this haven of peace and care.

Though Bucky remains cautious of human interaction, he is making daily progress, a testament to the patient and gentle love he receives from his caregivers. His story reminds us of God's faithfulness to all creatures, great and small.

"The Lord is good to all; He has compassion for all His creation."

— PSALM 145:9

REFLECTION

Bucky's journey from being lost and unwanted to finding a safe and loving home at Butterfly Field Farm mirrors the grace and mercy God extends to all of us. Just as He cares for the smallest of His creatures, God sees and values each one of us, offering redemption and new life. How can we reflect His love and compassion to the vulnerable and overlooked in our world?

PRAYER

Heavenly Father, thank You for Your unfailing love and care for all creation. We praise You for Bucky's story, which reminds us of Your mercy and provision. Help us to be faithful stewards of the animals You have entrusted to us, treating them with the kindness and compassion You demonstrate. May our actions reflect Your heart, bringing hope and healing to all who need it. In Jesus' name. Amen

Sweet little Bucky

TIMMY'S JOURNEY
TO GRACE AT BUTTERFLY FIELD FARM

"The eyes of the Lord are everywhere, keeping watch on the wicked and the good."

— PROVERBS 15:3

TIMMY, a Russian tortoise, is the newest resident of Butterfly Field Farm, where God's love and care extend to all creatures, great and small. At 8 years old and fully grown at 9 inches in diameter, Timmy has a remarkable life span of up to 200 years. In fact, Tara and Ted have to include Timmy in their will so that he will be passed down to the next generation and maybe even the generation after that. Insuring Timmy's future is the primary concern of the caregivers, so steps will be taken to know where he will go when Tara and Ted can no longer care for him. Timmy's journey to the sanctuary reflects God's compassion and provision. Having a reptile is a new experience for the sanctuary as Timmy is the very first of this kind to become a resident but was welcomed by all. One big happy family of many kinds, shapes and sizes.

Timmy's previous owners, facing a move, realized he wasn't thriving in his small tank. Proverbs 12:10 says:

"Good people take care of their animals, but even the kindest acts of the wicked are cruel."

They made the loving decision to find him a better home, so now he lives at Butterfly Field Farm. Timmy is cherished and cared for with the dignity and respect all God's creatures deserve. Bringing Timmy to the sanctuary posed new challenges, as cold-blooded animals like him require specialized care. Unable to regulate his body heat, Timmy needs a warm enclosure equipped with heat lamps when the weather is cold, and his diet must be carefully monitored to prevent overeating. These unique needs remind us of Matthew 6:26,

"Look at the birds in the sky. They do not plant or gather food or put it in houses. But your Father in heaven takes care of them."

In winter, Timmy stays cozy in his temperature-controlled home, a testament to God's provision. When summer comes, he will enjoy a spacious, predator-proof outdoor enclosure filled with grass to graze on and room to explore—an environment where he can thrive as God intended. Psalm 104:24-25 beautifully captures this vision:

"Lord, you have made many things. With Your wisdom, you made them all. The earth is full of what

You have made. The sea is so big and wide with animals large and small."

Cathy and Josh Sutherland, very dear friends of Tara and Ted's who live in Seminole, Florida, have a very large African Sulcata tortoise named Joey, who is 12 years old and weighs 60 pounds. He has a wonderful backyard to live in and his own house but loves to come inside their house to be with the family whenever he's allowed, especially when the nights get chilly. They purchased Joey when he was just a hatchling and didn't know his gender until he was 3 years old. Joey's main diet is grass, but every day, he gets additional treats like cucumbers, bell peppers, a head of Romaine lettuce, water-melon and strawberries. He doesn't drink water as he gets all the hydration he needs from the food he eats. He is very friendly and sociable and loves when you scratch and rub his shell and the top of his head. Turtles make awesome pets, even though they are different from cats or dogs, they are very sweet and loveable companions.

REFLECTION

Timmy's and Joey's story encourages us to reflect on our role as stewards of God's creation. How can we better care for the animals in our lives, ensuring they live the full and abundant life God desires for them? And even though Timmy is different, isn't it beautiful how he has been accepted by the residents of the farm. Wouldn't it be wonderful if we, as humans, could be like these beautiful animals of Butterfly Field Farm who live in such harmony. Such a wonderful lesson they teach us.

PRAYER

Dear Heavenly Father,

Thank You for the gift of animals and the opportunity to care for them as an expression of Your love. Help us to be wise stewards of Your creation, providing for the unique needs of each creature in our care. Bless Timmy, Joey and all the animals at Butterfly Field Farm, that they may live in peace and safety, reflecting Your goodness. Guide us to show kindness and compassion in all we do. In the precious Name of Jesus. Amen.

Sweet Little Timmy

Big Boy Joey

THE TALE OF THE BUTTERFLY FIELD DUCKS:
A STORY OF RESCUE AND REDEMPTION

BUTTERFLY FIELD FARM is a sanctuary of second chances, not just for the furry but for the feathered, too. Among our cherished residents are several ducks, each with their own story of rescue, renewal, and redemption.

The Duck Boys—Huey, Duey, and Louie—were our very first flock of ducks. They arrived from a woman who found herself overwhelmed with 14 male ducks. The aggressive fighting among the flock made it clear that a change was necessary, and so the Duck Boys found a safe home here at the farm.

Then came the Peking Ducks: Big Ricky, Little Ricky, Parker, and Laverne. Except for Laverne, all were abandoned in unsafe environments. Many people mistakenly believe that domestic ducks can survive in the wild, but they lack the ability to fend for themselves, such as the ability to fly. Domestic ducks can't get more than a few feet off the ground, so escaping a predator is a significant challenge. Laverne's story is unique—she was gifted to us by Tractor Supply Store as a companion to a rescued baby chick named

Shirley, as an unexpected friendship had blossomed into something beautiful. Laverne and Shirley were inseparable and were welcomed by everyone on the farm with open arms. As baby chick, Shirley grew into a full-grown chicken, she and Laverne remain close friends. Where you find one, the other is not far behind.

"A friend loves at all times, and a brother is born for a time of adversity."

— PROVERBS 17:17

From Laverne and Shirley to the bond shared by the wild siblings, true companionship thrives in unexpected places. Over time, our duck family grew, with more breeds and personalities adding to the joyful chaos on the farm. One of our standouts is Stevie, a duck with a knack for fun. Stevie is the only animal on the farm who uses the teeter-totter. He waddles up one side, waits for his weight to tip the board, then slides down the other side. Ted says it is a sight that will bring a smile and laughter to your soul.

A special story about Mr. Ping and Daisy, who were both disabled and could not walk. They came to the farm when their owners no longer could care for them. Both were beautiful white Peking ducks who lovingly sat side by side every day, keeping each other company. Ted would carry them out of their pen each morning and place them in the water trough to play, bathe and forget about their disability. When the duo was clean and ready to move, intense quacking would signal Ted to pluck them out of the water and place them on a soft bed of straw out in the sun to dry off and relax. There, they had food, water and the beauty of watching the other animals romp and play in the barnyard. At the end of the day, Tara and Ted would gently carry them back to their pen for the night, where they were safe and sound. Seeing the love between these two ducks was beautiful as well as the love their caregivers gave them. Sadly, both Mr. Ping and Daisy have passed, but they had the very best life possible in the loving arms of Tara and Ted.

"The Lord is good to all; He has compassion on all He has made."

— PSALM 145:9

Each duck's story reminds us that no life is beyond God's redemptive care.

We even had the privilege of raising five wild baby ducks whose mother was tragically killed the day they were hatched. At just five days old, they found refuge at Butterfly Field Farm from a good Samaritan. When they grew strong enough to fly, two left quickly, but three lingered, returning each afternoon for several months. Over time, only one continued visiting—Madelyn, the most vocal of the group. Her lively quacks often carried across the farm, bringing smiles to all who heard her. Madelyn is often absent from the farm for weeks at a time but has recently returned – with a boyfriend in tow!

Through these stories, we see God's hand in the lives of these ducks. He provides safe refuge, unlikely friendships, and moments of joy. Just as these ducks found a place to belong, so we too, find our place in His loving care.

"He will cover you with His feathers, and under His wings, you will find refuge."

— PSALM 91:4.

The sanctuary serves as a testament to God's promise to shelter and protect all who seek Him.

REFLECTION

Take a moment to reflect on the lives of the Butterfly Field Farm ducks. What can we learn from their stories of hope and renewal? Is there someone in your life who could use a helping hand or a kind word? How can you extend God's compassion to the creatures and people around you?

PRAYER

Heavenly Father, thank You for the lessons You teach us through Your creation. Just as You provide refuge and redemption for these ducks, we trust in Your care for us. Help us to be instruments of Your love, offering hope and compassion to all who cross our paths. May we always celebrate the joy found in Your creation. In Jesus' name, we pray. Amen

The 5 Abandoned Wild Ducks

Mr. Ping and Daisy

CHARLOTTE
A STORY OF BROKENNESS TO REDEMPTION

"For it is by grace you have been saved, through faith, and this is not from yourselves, it is the gift of God."

— EPHESIANS 2:8

IN MAY 2024, during early morning rush-hour, a trembling dog was put out of a car into the unforgiving traffic of Newport News, Virginia, at one of the busiest intersections in the city. With cars whizzing by, horns honking, and people screaming at her, this poor dog was spared only by the grace of God from being hit and killed. No one understands how she could have survived. Charlotte, at the time, was a one-year-old Labrador Retriever mix with a gleaming seal-like black coat that shimmers in the light and amazing golden eyes. A very beautiful girl with the sweetest personality but so fearful of everything because of her owner's cruelty. Abused and abandoned, this innocent soul faced a perilous fate. Yet, in the intricate tapestry of God's divine plan, a glimmer of hope emerged.

By the grace of God, she was rescued from the brink of death and sheltered within the walls of a local animal shelter. Though she bore no marks of identification, her plight stirred compassion in the hearts of those who cared for her. However, as the days turned into weeks, the shelter's resources dwindled, and the shadow of euthanasia loomed large.

But God had other plans. A beacon of hope appeared in the form of the Lab Rescue of Virginia, a dedicated organization committed to saving canine lives. They recognized the spark of life within this frightened creature and extended a lifeline, offering her a chance to heal and find a loving, forever home. Going from the Lab Rescue of Virginia to a foster family in Virginia, then finally to Butterfly Field Farm, Charlotte had found her way into loving arms, never to be abused again. The day Ted went to pick her up in Charlottesville, VA, she was on what is called her "Freedom Ride." Dog lovers freely give of their time, driving a rescue from volunteer to volunteer until they reach the pup's forever family. Praise God for the beautiful hearts of these special people who love dogs so very much to help them in this selfless way.

Butterfly Field Farm, a haven of peace and tranquility, became her sanctuary. Ted and Tara, with their gentle hearts and unwavering love, embraced her with open arms. Though she remained wary, their patience and persistence began to chip away at her fear. As days turned into weeks, a transformation unfolded, a testament to the power of love and the grace of God. Tara's parents, Susan and Larry Randolph had lost their beloved Gracie the year before, a white British lab who was almost 15 years old. She had been such a huge part of their lives, and they needed time to mourn, but now were ready to bring another dog into their family. They also have Sadie, a white British lab who is 7 years old from the same bloodline as Gracie. Sadie was very lonely since her big sister passed so it was time to seriously begin looking for a companion for both the humans and canine in the household. Susan and Larry knew they wanted a rescue dog to give a beautiful, loving forever home, so when Charlotte came to Butterfly Field Farm, Tara told her parents that she would be the perfect dog for them. Only God could bring the perfect dog into their lives all the way from Newport News, Virginia. Their hearts yearned for a loyal friend, and God, in His infinite wisdom, led them to this precious soul. With their gentle white Lab, Sadie, by their side, they formed a perfect match, a family destined to love and cherish this once lost pup.

As the adoption day dawned, a sense of peace and joy filled the air. The once-frightened pup, now bathed in love and hope, embarked on a new chapter, a journey of endless possibilities. For God had not only saved her life but had also woven her into a beautiful tapestry of love and redemption. As the scripture says:

"The Lord is good to all, and his tender mercies are over all his works."

— PSALM 145:9

REFLECTION

Charlotte's journey mirrors the redemptive love God offers to all creation. Just as she was saved from the brink of death, we, too, are rescued by God's compassion and grace. The Bible declares:

> "He heals the brokenhearted and binds up their wounds."

> — PSALM 147:3

In her new life, Charlotte reflects the truth of Romans 8:28,

> "And we know that in all things God works for the good of those who love Him."

PRAYER

Heavenly Father, thank You for Your tender mercies and unwavering compassion. You care for all Your creation, even the smallest and most vulnerable. Thank You for rescuing Charlotte and placing her in a family that will love and cherish her all the days of her life. Help us to see opportunities to extend Your grace to those in need, whether human or animal. May we always reflect Your love in our actions, offering redemption and hope to the broken and hurting. In the precious name of Jesus, we pray. Amen

Beautiful Charlotte

EPILOGUE

As HUMAN BEINGS, we share a deep connection with animals. Their vulnerability touches our hearts, and witnessing their suffering brings us profound sadness. We struggle to comprehend cruelty inflicted upon these defenseless creatures.

Throughout these pages, we've journeyed through stories of resilience and redemption, each a testament to the power of hope. We've witnessed the plight of Susie and Gerry, two donkeys rescued from the horrors of a kill pen, deprived of food, water, and hope. Their story, like so many others, reminds us of the desperate circumstances animals can face. Yet, through divine intervention and human compassion, they found salvation.

We've mourned the tragedy of abandoned farm animals left to starve, a stark reminder of the neglect that can leave innocent lives shattered. In the face of such despair, we've also celebrated the unwavering spirit of those who survived, finding new beginnings and loving homes.

The story of the young steer who lost his sight due to

neglect underscores the importance of responsible care. His vulnerability highlights the crucial role compassionate individuals play in intervening and offering a lifeline to those in need.

Now, picture Butterfly Field Farm, a sanctuary nestled in the rolling hills at the foot of the Blue Ridge Mountains. Imagine this haven as a place of healing, where these rescued animals find refuge, love, and the promise of a peaceful life. Here, they are cherished, protected, and finally experience the joy of belonging.

These 21 stories, collected in "Miracles in the Meadow Butterfly Field Farm Devotional, The True Inspiring Stories of Rescue and Redemption," are more than just tales of animals. They are reflections of God's redemptive grace, mirroring the love and forgiveness we ourselves have received. Just as these animals have been given a second chance, so too have we all been redeemed by the boundless love of our Heavenly Father.

It is our hope that these stories have touched your heart and deepened your understanding of the profound connection we share with all living beings. May they serve as a reminder that love, especially the unwavering love of our Lord, Jesus Christ, truly conquers all.

CALL TO ACTION:

Inspired by the stories you've read, we invite you to join us in making a difference in the lives of animals in need, both at Butterfly Field Farm and beyond. There are many ways you can get involved:

AT BUTTERFLY FIELD FARM:

- **Visit Butterfly Field Farm:** Experience the sanctuary firsthand and witness the transformative power of compassion. Contact us at: www.butterflyfieldfarm.org. 1327 Ryan Estates Lane, Bedford, VA. 24523. Email: info@butterflyfieldfarm.org.
- **Donate to Butterfly Field Farm:** Your generous contributions directly support the food, shelter, veterinary care, and ongoing needs of the rescued animals at Butterfly Field Farm. Go to www. butterflyfieldfarm.org and click on Donate or mail a check to 1327 Ryan Estates Lane, Bedford, VA 24523. Learn how to sponsor an animal by going to Animal Sponsorship | Butterfly Field Farm for information.
- A percentage of the net royalties will be made as a love donation to Butterfly Field Farm by the author.

- **Volunteer at Butterfly Field Farm:** Share your time and talents by volunteering at the sanctuary. Opportunities may include animal care, grounds maintenance, administrative support, and event assistance at www.butterfieldfarm.org and click on Volunteer Contact Information/Link.
- **Support Local Animal Shelters and Rescues:** Consider donating to or volunteering at animal shelters and rescue organizations in your own community. These organizations provide vital services to animals in need.
- **Advocate for Animal Welfare:** Speak out against animal cruelty and support legislation that protects animals.
- **Practice Responsible Pet Ownership:** If you have pets, ensure they receive proper care, including regular veterinary checkups, nutritious food, and a safe and loving environment.
- **Spread the Word:** Share these stories and information about animal welfare with your friends, family, and social networks to raise awareness and inspire others to take action.
- **Pray:** Continue to pray for the well-being of all animals, for the individuals and organizations dedicated to their care, and for an end to animal suffering.

By acting on the compassion these stories have ignited within you, you become part of the ongoing story of healing, hope, and redemption, not only at Butterfly Field Farm but throughout the world.

Acknowledgments

To God, my Father,

Thank You for touching my heart and inspiring me to write this book. Your Word has been my guide and comfort, especially the promise in Proverbs 3:5-7,

"Trust in the Lord with all your heart; do not depend on your own understanding. Seek His will in all you do, and He will show you which path to take."

This scripture has been a cornerstone of my life, and I am humbled by how You have blessed my obedience and trust in You through the creation of this book.

Father, thank You for entrusting me with the opportunity to share these beautiful stories of hope, love, redemption, and grace. Your sacrificial love, reflected in the lives of Tara, Ted, and the amazing animals of Butterfly Field Farm, is a testament to Your compassion for all of creation.

I love You, Father, and dedicate this work to Your glory. May it always point to Your boundless love and faithfulness.

To Ted and Tara,

Thank you for your unwavering commitment and boundless love for the animals of Butterfly Field Farm. Your sanctuary is a place of hope and healing, where lives are redeemed from the brink of despair. Through your tireless dedication and 24/7 care, you have created a haven where God's love and grace are evident in every life you touch.

The stories of these gentle and sweet souls are a testament to your kindness and compassion. Many will find inspiration in the lives you have transformed and the journeys you have shared. Never doubt that you are deeply appreciated and loved by all who follow your remarkable mission.

May God bless you abundantly as you continue your faithful and diligent care of His beautiful creatures. We love you and stand in awe of all you do.

To my amazing wife and life partner, Susan,

This book would not have been possible without your unwavering love, support, and understanding. Your deep appreciation for Butterfly Field Farm and its many animals has inspired every story within these pages. Your keen eye for detail has brought vivid descriptions of this beautiful sanctuary nestled in the Blue Ridge Mountains to life, allowing readers to experience its captivating stories firsthand.

Your profound wisdom and understanding of scripture has been integral to shaping the heart of this book. Together, we have woven God's love, grace, and redemption into each story, presenting a collection that reflects His care for all creation.

Susan, your participation has been invaluable, and I am deeply grateful for every moment you have poured into this labor of love. I love you beyond measure.

Forever yours,
    Larry

About the Author

Larry Randolph, author of Finding Grace, the 2024 Best Book Awards Winner in the nonfiction/animal category by American Book Fest, shares true and inspiring stories of hope, love, obedience and redemption. His award-winning book chronicles the extraordinary impact of therapy dogs in bringing comfort and healing to a hurting world.

In 2007, he founded an international faith-based therapy dog organization supported by hundreds of dedicated volunteers throughout the world. As a Community Chaplain and Board Certified Crisis Response Specialist, Larry brings comfort and encouragement to those in need, visiting cancer centers, special needs facilities, and nursing homes alongside his beloved therapy dog, Sadie.

Together with his wife and ministry partner, Susan, Larry resides in Lutz (Tampa), Florida, where they cherish their role as parents to four wonderful daughters and grandparents to nine beloved grandchildren. When not ministering to others, Larry finds joy in spending time with family, including Sadie, their 7 year old English Labrador Retriever. After the passing of their beloved therapy dog Gracie in 2023, they have recently rescued and adopted Charlotte, a beautiful black Labrador Retriever mix. She is one year old and has been terribly abused, but has now joined our family and will be safe and loved for the rest of her life. We feel God brought her to us all the way from Newport News, Virginia and we feel very blessed.

Larry and Susan are active in several Bible study groups, volunteers at Metropolitan Ministries and members of Bay Hope Church and are continually seeking to deepen their knowledge of God's Word and grow in their relationship with their Heavenly Father. Through their ministry and daily lives, they strive to reflect God's grace, love, and compassion —values that shine brightly in the stories of Butterfly Field Farm.

Larry can be reached at www.findinggrace15@gmail.com or the website www.findinggrace15.com.

CREDITS

Unless otherwise noted, all photographs within this book are the property of Butterfly Field Farm, and all rights are reserved.

All scripture is taken from the New Living Version and New International Version of the Holy Bible.

www.ingramcontent.com/pod-product-compliance
Lightning Source LLC
Chambersburg PA
CBHW070843160726

48004CB00001B/486